Accordion Breathing and Dancing

ACCORDION BREATHING AND DANCING

Ruth L. Schwartz

University of Pittsburgh Press

The publication of this book is supported by a grant from the Pennsylvania Council on the Arts.

Published by the University of Pittsburgh Press, Pittsburgh, Pa. 15260
Copyright © 1996, Ruth L. Schwartz
All rights reserved
Manufactured in the United States of America
Printed on acid-free paper

This book is the winner of the 1994 Associated Writing Programs' award series in poetry. Associated Writing Programs, a national organization serving over 150 colleges and universities, has its headquarters at George Mason University, Tallwood House, Mail Stop 1E3, Fairfax, Va. 22030

Library of Congress Cataloging-in-Publication Data

Schwartz, Ruth L., 1962–
Accordion breathing and dancing / Ruth L. Schwartz.
    p. cm. —(Pitt Poetry Series)
   ISBN 0-8229-3898-7 (cl.).—ISBN 0-8229-5571-7 (pbk.)
   I. Title. II. Series.
PS3569.C56738A23   1995   95-30750
811'.54—dc20   CIP

A CIP catalogue record for this book is available from the British Library.
Eurospan, London

Book design: Frank Lehner

for Gladys

Contents

I

When They Know	5
Poems of the Body	6
The man speaks	8
When you in your sturdy and luminous body	10
Finally, there is your lust	11
I keep coming back to this longing	12
By Asking	13
The Small Outlined Against the Large	14
Grief	18

II

The City	23
These Streets	25
The City at Sunset	26
Market Street	29
AIDS Education, Seventh Grade	30
Night Pieces	32

III

In the Country of the Flesh	39
Scene with Pelicans	41
January Vineyards	42
Bath	43
Risk	44
The Offering	45
And the Light	46
Near us, a new house	47
Triptych: Grizzly Peak	48
August, Early Evening	50

IV

Near Your Death, a Visit	53
Letter from Anywhere	55
Foreigner	57
In the Time of Plague	58
In Another Country	59
Late Monologue for a Traveler	65
Cirque du Soleil	67

V

Possible	71
In Guatemala	72
Language Lesson	73
Almolonga Market	74
History	75
The Twelfth Day of Christmas	79
Late Summer	80
The Greatest Show on Earth	81

Accordion Breathing and Dancing

I

When They Know

—FOR H., WHO TESTED POSITIVE

*"The man sitting next to Susan just disappeared,"
said one passenger.—News item, February 25, 1989*

We are talking about the plane:
the nine who followed the fuselage,
the sky which sucked them up lit by the jet's parts going up,
debris storming the hole—
the three hundred and forty-six who remained,
firmly buckled in their seats,
bolted to the floor, fused
to the wings and frame.

And it is not surprising that I think mostly of
the three hundred and forty-six:
their lives gleaming ahead of them,
some of them turning to religion, others finally able to love,
how they will continue belting themselves
into their seats, as if it keeps them safe,
how they will think there is some reason they survived—

while you can't stop thinking about the nine:
those few, randomly plucked from their lives,
radiance hurtling into dark—
you are with them in that instant,
just when they know they are leaving

Poems of the Body

1

That night in the hot tub,
in the faraway house-light,
I saw your penis gleaming in its mat of hair
unraveled like the straw they use for packing melons,
sending them long distances; I looked away.
I do not know your body, only cell-counts, lives
beneath your skin, and what multiplies in them
which is not you, not of you, but a stranger nodding silently
between our sentences,
bored as a child who, all through the lengthy
dinner, waits to be excused.

2

In the photograph, your cells
are bunched like snow on branches, furred blue globes
while from their stumpy twigs the virus spreads
golden and red, unseasonal,
rapid as multiflora rose—
those destroying, blooming arms.

In the shared, immoral heart of science and poetry,
all things are beautiful:
evolution or mutation,
wanted or unwanted change
unstoppable, the body's blameless gaze

The knowledge of death throws open our windows

We stand here seeing, eating light

3

Watching you sleep,
what I see is no more, no less than any stranger could:
your face as close to me as sand, the breathing dune of neck,
black needlepoints of light, your shaven cheek,
hands still as nests, opening where they lie,

and I do not know whether or not it helps me to love you,
looking so closely at you,
whether I love you *in* this body, or through, or
completely apart from it,

your life encoded in each eyelash, every cell,

and in the air between us now,

and in all things which will outlive you

The man speaks

—with thanks to Eric Jasmen

       slowly,
             slowly.
He is thirty-three
and his mind
stops,
has to push-
     start itself
after almost
     every
        word

           except when a smooth phrase suddenly
           tumbles, slick with joy

He has come to tell us
it is possible to live with dementia,

to live not knowing if today
he will remember how to read,
   or will not.

If it is the mind I love,
   but it is not only the mind,

  if it is the body I love,
     but have never touched,

      is there another name for what
         of you I love

in this daily disappearing, where the sky
    and water can be kept

When You in Your Sturdy and Luminous Body

tell me you are starting to prepare for death,
you say it as if you are facing a window, and so, quite naturally,
   you are looking out,

and the view is enormous,

   the storm has furrowed green the grass,
     yellow the fields of sour-grass,
        sky opening to water shining
          with its swallowed sun—

I look in gulps, then look away—

   women and men in white tights swimming flips through air,
     pole on the forehead of a man on tightrope,
        woman balanced on the pole,
          gymnast on his hands clasped
             to the raised hands of his lover,

love as the moment of not knowing,
recognizing the loved other as completely *other*, unknowable,

   then water like a field of snow, the sun skating a path,
     fiery edges—the clouds' skin
        made golden

and I do not know how to answer you
but by seeing

Finally, there is your lust

which failed to keep you alive,
but which did not kill you,
no matter what you say.
Lust glowing in you like a burnt
cathedral—and you toured its ruins,
sweating and marveling . . .

And then the flesh like light
forked from your spine.
This man half-blind,
unable to reach his food-
he isn't you.
If I never see you again,

Brazil has taken you back.
All night in the smoky heat,
mouthing the Portuguese like song.
Watching the chubby drag queen ride
the railing, a greased horse . . .
Clapping, you swim through air.

I keep coming back to this longing

to be larger than my life.
To do something more than go on day by day
within the limits of my understanding:

AZT's four-hour clock,

the lovely buttered bodies of the disappearing men

who in loving each other are loving, not death
but the life which rises to meet it, when it must,
just as the land's edge seems to tilt
raising itself to meet the sky
and the sky settles thick as a heavy snow
into the body's crevices—

the sand striated with the branching tracks of birds

my life planted among the falling lives

By Asking

—for Ron

To love, one must ask for everything.—Otto René Castillo

Then there were three hours more of waiting with the body
he had become—a body, no longer your friend, your four years' lover,
and in that room you and his mother said the things which you
would keep
    beyond that time,
storytelling, promising, crying, remembering,
so he, though dead, was still a conduit of love.

The love which brings us here, which lets us go,
until wherever we find ourselves, even in these fluorescent rooms,
we feel the vastness close to us, the ragged ocean's edge.
Tonight it is low tide; I walk far out on the wet glistening,
my shoes unhurried, without fear.
There is no moon; the light comes from the waves themselves,

swollen, salty, and luminous,
returning again and again to the same the changed shore.
                      If we ask for everything,
we are enlarged by asking, when grief opens us,
and what we do not understand becomes a way of turning
toward each other, and what we cannot say becomes a reason
    for speaking,
until, finally, everything has been said.

The Small Outlined Against the Large

—for C.K.H. (1957-1987)

1

I have so little left of you:
six poems you published at twenty-three,
thirty-odd pages from a novel
you gave up on, which I scavenged
from your trash the following week,
along with two drafts of a letter
your father would never receive.
I have one note you left
on the table, asking for a copy
of our shared key,
one clipping you stuck on our refrigerator
that year, and a tape of one record you loved.
I have no photographs of you,
but I do have a letter from your father
(retired U.S. Air Force Colonel
Charles W. Hinkle, Sr.)
thanking me for my card of sympathy.
I have nothing else that was yours
except what you have lodged in me:
tapping the bone between my breasts
like your uneven typewriter.
I rub my fingertips against the spot,
feeling its smallness, commonness:
old friend who has become a scar,
reading my poems before I write them,
pouring me more pink wine.

2

Then there's the sex
I never had with you,
passed like a glowing
bowl on the table
between us, without our touching it,
like an inspired pointer on a Ouija board
reaching its cryptic messages
under our hands.
The table was yours.
It was made of teak:
rich, light wood,
perfectly round.
We drew our poems
from crumpled paper bags,
read them aloud, tilting
the jug of wine till 3 A.M.
Another night we danced,
pretending tropics in December,
turning the thermostat on high:
you in your tiny red satin shorts,
me in my slit purple skirt,
laughing as we burnt a month's heat.

3

Daily, when I check your weather,
straining to see your house
under its hill of fog,
thinking of you as I last saw you,
eager dog pawing your chest,
the way your hands, knobby and trembling
as an old man's, braced against the wall
to hold you up under that love,

and how you stood there, wasted
face the wrong size for your bones,
the ruby fleck piercing your eye,
and blew a kiss to me with just your lips,
no hands, the way you always did,

I do not believe you are dead.
I am too used to watching the sky
over your part of the city,
as when we lived together, turning onto
our street, I'd check for your old red truck
and when you left, I'd watch the truck
move down the silent, shady road,
its white Virginia license gleaming
like a single tooth.

4

The clams are breathing beneath the sand.
Through its packed surface,
airholes burst like eyes.
There are thousands of them,
each one separate, yet part of many,
the small outlined against the large,
stretching the beach for miles . . .
This is what grief is like,
all sizes at once,
because there is no such thing as a single grief,
because we do not live singly;
the place in my life you have left
is smaller than a fingernail
and larger than the whole of my body.
I walk this beach pockmarked by clams,
whole cities of them, breathing underground,
remembering your death is one
among thousands,
remembering you bristling,
tender and particular,
twirling the kitchen in your cowboy boots,
stirring the garlic soup that could cure anything.

Grief

Tonight a man with AIDS called,
threatened to set himself on fire
in front of our office next week
unless somebody does something.
Goddamnit, someone
do
something.

Sometimes I want to kill you
before the virus can.

I'm getting tired of loving people
who are someday going to die. I'd like
another kind to love—angels maybe,
starched and virtuous. All those gauzy wings!
Or maybe the already-dead,
    no surprises there . . .

I want to take you to the airport,
wave to a blurred face, a tiny hand
while the huge plane roars.
At least that one goodbye would be distinct,
    comprehensible

❖

There is nothing now which death does not enter
Sex, the unnamed forest fire
That hour between us like a lit match

❖

Yet how joy surges, sometimes, at death's lip
when there are no more reasons *not* to live

II

The City

—in memory of Ariel Jiménez

*That was my dream. Just to walk down the street, holding hands
with another man.*—Andy

Saint Francis in his brown robe in the garden honors
every butterfly and bird, every living thing,
and in the city named for him,
where *gay* is a spoken language,
even the trim on the gingerbread houses
dances with color, up and down the hills
to the ocean, the very edge of the world we know.
And it is not the city itself which is killing the pretty men,
though because they came here from anywhere else,
Mexico, Colombia, Grenada, Puerto Rico,
Cleveland, Milwaukee, Nashville, desperation,
all lured by the echo of open kisses,
because they came here with blood and bodies unpoisoned,
and will fall here, most of them,
straitjacketed by IV tubes,
oxygen nosepieces, stainless steel bed walls,
it is hard not to think,
if they had not come here,
they would have survived.
I am driving one of them to the hospital
and still the others stride toward us, against the light,
their butterfly faces, their perfect apple asses,
their hands in each others' hands, while the oldies
station plays Dylan knock-knock-knocking on heaven's door.
We all came here from somewhere else,
but because we know this city,
because we chose it like a lover, winding our lives

through its streets as if caressing them,
we imagine the city knows *us*,
recognizes us
in its invisible heart,
even as death pats its hands
around the sand of our bodies
as if sculpting us, and we open
our mouths to the tide.

THESE STREETS

—after a Sunday shooting

Where we go out into the world
armed only with our bodies—which are not armor

Sail on in our damaged bodies,
seeing by the sudden, tender flaring-up of light

Carmine, scarlet, burgundy
Blood from the bodies of wet roses

At each moment, everything
is being handed to us

The stories course like foam from lips
of broken bottles, crazy to be told

The green, half-eaten apple flashes brassy teeth
in the man's hand, sprawled on the shattered ground

A woman's clean hair lilts over her shoulders
as she walks—joy would be that brave

The City at Sunset

Outside the hospital, daylight is softening
under the sky's weight, pale orange as the inside
of a ripe plum, and, later, blue as the plum's skin.
The fog shifts on the hill, speared and vigilant.
It's that kind of dusk when everything

makes music—
even the dirty bus leaving the curb:
an enormous, wheezing music.
The sharp buildings are etched in light.
They turn their vacant faces toward the sun.
Behind them, dark fog billows

like a fire which will never overtake them.
The beggar on Sixteenth Street removes his prosthesis.
The place where his knee ends is dark and rounded
as a baby's head.
How innocent they look, the plastic toes,

naked on the piss-soaked street.
This little piggy went to market . . .
Once, even the piss was beautiful,
streaming in its golden arc,
warm as winter sun.

When you truly love a city, or a body,
everything is possible

There are people lying in its streets,
but still you believe.
There are organs failing in the breath's nest
of cells, but still—

You do not mean to forgive
that which should not be forgiven,
you mean to see everything,
but still the love spills out of you
like vision, like diamonds

How beautiful it looks, the new fruit in wooden bins
on the corner where the shots were heard,
the lemons gleaming like waxed moons,
nectarines' skins flaming with promise.
In the street, paramedics are loading a man

into their flashing truck.
Just before his body disappears, he sits up,
unfurling on the stretcher like a brown, dried leaf.
Even his hands are slowly opening.

Under the flimsy hospital vest
the landscape of your body,
arms which I have curved against the bed
like twin moons.

Between my teeth, your nipples
pucker into stars.

The ravaged city, glittering,
spreads open before me,
before anyone who will look.

Do you know what this world asks of us?

Watching the doctor's hand move toward your breast,
dispassionate, medical hand,
interested only in the heart

failing beneath your skin,
I try to imagine how it would feel
not to love you,

not to look through the opened window
where the sky in its flamingo colors waits,

where every night the moon rides,
shines its honeysuckle cream,
funnels the light of the world into our bodies.

If we are not our bodies, what are we?

Look, each step is a dance step
to the man lurching across the street
on his rotten leg,
and each life goes on glittering
against the vast, bruised, city landscape,

goes on in its movements like ocean,
whether we look or not.

Someone has broken into the sky,
scooped out pink curds of cloud
and scattered them

Deeper we go with open mouths

Market Street

―for J. M. (1958–1994) and K. L.

Flag-rainbows lofted over canyons,
those spots of view where anyone can stand
to love the whole world

Every life-form canny and exuberant

The scarlet bougainvillea
bursting like flame through fences
Lesions like burnished fire
spreading on the skin

The sweet shoulder blades of the
high school girls
bared in halter tops
in the rare heat

Brilliant sunset issuing from fog,
its shot-through clarity
The Castro cast in light and dark
like a diorama
The big Safeway sign
etched on orange cloud

The light falls, at this moment, on
John and Keith
A doctor says, Cryptosporidium, Sarcoma
John says, We adore each other
The big imported palm trees,
newly planted, gaily wave their fronds
We gaze up at their hula dance
There are so many other things
that don't matter

―San Francisco, summer 1993

AIDS Education, Seventh Grade

—for M. M.

*This poem follows the sequence of the three-day AIDS
education program provided in many Bay Area schools.*

Day 1—AIDS Overview

The children are blooming like black flowers,
their teeth are white and lovely, it doesn't matter
what country they live in, the dying
moves over them like wind
through the captured fields.
When I ask how many know someone with AIDS
they all shout, their arms rising like snakes,
waving hungry palms,
can a dog get it, can you get it from a hickey,
did it come from red monkeys,
why can't they just pump out all a person's blood
and put in new?
Afterward the teacher says to me, That one there,
buck teeth, she has sex with three or four boys a week,
they come over from the high school,
do it to her in the yard,
her sister had a baby at thirteen—

                                              and overhead, the dark

bodies of the hawks
riding their hunger through the clear sky,
the sun laying its fair, long tongue
over everything.

Day 2—A Speaker with AIDS

One-third of the class speaks no English
and Mark of the beautiful Indian cheekbones,
the barrio, the broken, winged life
stumbles in his grandparents' Spanish
so the solemn little freckled kid translates
as Mark says, Tell them it's going to kill me,
saying, *Dice que lo va a matar,*
his dark-lashed sunflower face composed

and the sun says, Forget about the forty days
and nights of rain, I'm here, I'm burning

Day 3—You Must Protect Yourself

It's like shouting from the shore
of a glittering lake,
Look, we've been given these bodies
we don't understand,
we could spend our whole lives
learning how to live in them.

It doesn't matter what I say.

Sex, if it hasn't already, will rise up in them
like something from another world,
like the snowy egret on its perfect stilts
in the dank puddle by the highway,
shocking in its grace,
fishing for its life

Night Pieces

    1

Flesh leaping like a sleek cat
through decaying rooms

The hunger and the spirit
not strangers to each other

Your clitoris against my tongue
like a rage of wings

As if the night could dream us broken
birds made whole

    2

Your desire leads me
like the sound of water

and your death like something
bobbing on the far-off sheen, we can't tell
its shape—is it a log?
a bird? a small boat?
nor when it will reach us.

In the deep, there is room for everything
Shocked into motion
Lulled to dreamy ice

Meanwhile the water strokes the sand
like this, you say, moving your hand,
así, así.

3

The boats lined up like messengers
People in the water like dark flowers
in a field of light

Falling like music,
the blue, stolen light

The water luminous as memory
around the stones

Its will to make sense of everything

4

The unstifled cry in the dark room,
the bed which in one moment holds
a universe, then gives us back,

invisible shower of sparks, sweat,
more than could ever be used,
gorgeous excess, so much heat and gleam
no one could hoard,

as if all the lost, discarded dreams
could startle up like bits of dark
which then are seen to be a flock of birds

5

These birds, or others
Reasons to live, or not to

The way the wings
are lungs, filling the sky with breath

Quality of light which creeps
orange and unasked
between the downtown skyscrapers

The body, ordinary, naked
The robe removed

Each note rung like a diamond
through still air

   6

Night, the time which doesn't end,
the sleeper rustling upstairs
through a hidden life, bed of dreams
despite the cramped, twisting feet and hands
to which the blood's journey
is no longer faithful.

Downstairs the fire
reimagining itself
reconfigures hunger around each new log.

Forgiveness is only part of the story
the dead bring in dreams,
gathering everyone who is still alive
like flames sucked into one coal

   7

On the night's rainy wings, I drive and drive
The all-night drugstore, faces I don't see

A skidded curve, the black, empty road
Lights tiny with the lost day

Lungs which breathed light in and shrank it
to this violence

Your ribs exhausted with it
Only one of many dangers

Still day will come around with its bright face
The sky washed impossibly clean

   8

As if there were no other self,
desire like a fig tree with its crooked limbs,
its branches wild with fruit,
restlessness like the tiny feet of flies
landing on my skin

As if I did not love everywhere at once,
faithful to another country's streets
at the same time, nights, that I lift the quilt
beside my sleeping life

   9

The way the lights of any city
wait for your life to happen among them,
glowing like the field's corn,
beauty and worms hidden together,
all the rows you could get lost in

Planes like angels coasting to the ground
with their wings on fire,

church bells like a child's heart
praising every quarter hour

Even the sweat loving the skin
Even the bubbled stream of urine
as it soaks the curb

Even the birds, if you look,
only fill your throat with something
which seems to have no place to land—
how the sky holds them in their rightful place,
how they hold the sky

III

In the Country of the Flesh

When the catheter bag on my leg continues filling itself
with warm, unwilled urine,
I think about the price we pay to be made of flesh,
the pain that sails us through the flooded streets

where upstream, women wash pigs' entrails
and the sheeps' mouths mutter rainlike
over new grass.

I buckle sandals on your ruined feet
We walk beside the gleaming sea,
dreamy iguanas gumming lettuce with their prehistoric mouths,
old women with machetes hacking coconuts,
armies of lovely, drunken tourists
sagging in the heat.

Now the land prepares itself for rain.
The dark roosters scratch the ground and sing.
The fronds of coconut grow fierce.
The frogs pause, listening.
Even the clouds, which had grown tired,
are rising from the hills where they had rested
and the landscape billows upward,
rippling its fingers through the flesh of sky.

We drive the old, open car through mountains
while the fog's many faces pray for us.

The lizards' tiny, pinkish hands appear on every wall.
Even the gutter-puddles swarm with fish.
The sand pulses under us,
the tiny clams are dancing to the surface, ravenous,
opening their jellied bodies, pale as moon.
They eat until the water buries them,
their starshaped mouths still puckering

You bring me your country's fruits:
quenepa, piña, passion fruit,
guayaba, fourteen kinds of mango.
At night the bushes fill with egrets,
sleeping between the branches like white leaves,
while the stars above us fall in love
with the stars below us, the lucid waters
glowing, even in our hands.

I used to see the stars, you say
your eyes crosshatched by laser scars,
the brilliant retina unmooring from its dark, still pool

Coal-colored birds hover beside the scarlet bougainvillea
Their wings move faster than sight
The flowers are flaming, they want so badly
to be remembered

Scene with Pelicans

They are everywhere, the pelicans,
in what could be the last year of your life,
passing the brief fringe of their enormous wings
within bare inches of the water,
pumping like a child's legs on swings
above us, in formation,
conducting orchestras of wind.
The legs of our table are planted in sand;
at dusk we watch the tied boats darken
while the crazy woman bathes,
dressed, in the brown salt water,
and the pelicans dive histrionically,
downward right-angle midflight turns,
waving their awkward little feet.
It almost doesn't matter that they reappear,
necks stretched with fish.
Behind them, the sky is breaking open.

January Vineyards

How our bodies fail to confine our longings,
even in death's season, withholding nothing

How the hills furrow like a cherished body,
leaning into the opened hand of the lake

How the brittle grapevines braid the fields

How the vagina clenches, prayerfully,
around the fingers which have entered it

How the canopy of leaves will bless the fruit,
each grape soft and ready for the mouth

>   Sex was going to be the landscape
>   which would make our bodies perfect,
>   and it has

How savagely I want you, even here,
on the white stretcher, in the pallid hospital

BATH

Through the hot water, your belly,
your lovely, fat, floating, abused belly,
flesh you stick with daily needles
which bruises, sometimes, into purple blossom.
Desire branches there teeth-first,
taking us both.
Love, to describe you
perhaps I should start with your feet,
scaly and nerveless, toenails gone,
flesh crusted-over in their place.
Under your skin the kidneys bloat, helpless to let go
the long, clean, clear streams of urine,
and when you walk a block, or up a flight of stairs,
your arteries choke shut and airless,
panting on their tracks—
how far away it seems, that castle,
your struggling heart.
Sometimes you look to me like an old woman,
despairing and fat.
Still, your breasts float toward me,
hot, wet, buoyant moons
I can hold in my two hands,
and still, when we gather each other,
rolling and sliding into sudden, holy want,
the body says *Revere me,*
                                  and I do.

Risk

All right, the wind
holding its breath

Teeth stunning each other.
Nipple. Tongue

Even if it means the green
plums will be blown from branches

The Offering

I am trying in your language
to explain the force beyond our knowing—
*La fuerza que hace volver
las cosas a la tierra,* I say, defining gravity,
after the bad news from the hospital,
and still, when I touch you anywhere,
lay even a lone finger on your arm, we turn translucent

with desire—like the blue-hazed eye of any
newborn, or the jeweled snake as it prepares to shed,
and though it cannot stop your crying, nor my leaving,
nor the dying of your brother, nor the virus blooming
in his cells,

each time we touch again, the conversation of our skin resumes
exactly where we left it last.
We are, we are, our bodies say,
my arms a nest you fill completely,
your large, mortal fingers bringing me
as if orgasm were a place, unimaginably beautiful,

and surrounded by impassable cliffs.
Into this canyon of astonishment, we plunge,
racing the disappearing light—
no, not the light itself, but its disappearance,
as the body's long tongue leans to catch
                                        each falling offering

And the Light

As your brother lies dying in the front room, and the scent
of his shit rises up through the house, and the light
continues helplessly to pour itself through our bodies,
I need you rough,
need you to swear to me with teeth and fingernails
desire can overtake the force of death.
When we wake again, he is still dying.
Relentlessly light funnels through us, between us, we are
    swimming in it.
The body's river will take everything.

Near Us, a New House

being built; for weeks the steady hammering, the lip-
vibrating saw like conversations we aren't
having yet, and then the silence of the bones
revealed. How little we can know the one
we say is loved, the one who shelters us;
each day seeming so final now,
lights on their timers coming on
all up and down the block like fingers
tapping on an empty glass.
The moon grows blurry in the sky;
its face is being eaten away
or maybe it is being reconstructed; from this distance
rock upon creviced rock, we cannot tell

Triptych: Grizzly Peak

1

The morning is gray.
The sky   the pavement
everything born and risen in the same shade

until suddenly, as if someone had arranged it,
the children run out into the gray schoolyard
wearing their bodies like wings,
their jackets redder and pinker and more orange
than the very flame of the imagination

which the world is always extinguishing
and reigniting, in every instant,
without intending to.

2

Anything, as you hold it, becomes both more and less precious

The vast lightfield spread before you,
seen from the ridge of your own life,
magnificent to the stranger who has only just
happened upon this road,
dulling to your eyes

Even the clear sky of someone's face
which once you discovered
with an astronomer's excitement
like a new star

Below you, there are streets you know as well
as your own body,

a band of light so narrow
it scarcely contains you,
so wide
    you can't see its shores

  3

The clouds are so big
in the distance, they must love you

and the fluttering of many birds
moves like a single wing
against the open space of your body.

Who ever lived who didn't want
more than their life?

But you are here, exactly here
in this sensate body
in this rain
and so you hold them,
the bright-coated children

pouring
       like a human river
into the gray arroyo of day

August, Early Evening

    Through the hot sky
the swallows move,
    dark, and then beneath their wings the light,
longing, that familiar storm.
    The ice-cream truck
jingles its ragtime tunes.
    Even the unmade bed
holds a sweetness.
    Wind takes the clouds
like children in its mouth.
    We love the moving sky. We love our lives.

IV

Near Your Death, a Visit

We talk about longing,
about all the lives our bodies
have abandoned

Your apartment is lovely as a nest
Carved wood above the entry way,
purple and yellow irises, just beginning
to wilt on the mantle

I memorize it all
as if it will burn to the ground when I leave

Outside the five-sided window, pigeons rise straight up,
immune to gravity.
Your sleek black cat is watching,
every muscle tensed.

We agree there is nothing to do about the longing.
All things are astounding to the memory,
which wanders in a land of brilliant windows

so you find yourself, for a moment,
on the Greek sand,
or smuggled into a soldier's barracks
in Istanbul—
his narrow hips, his narrow bed
The way he'd wake you in the darkness, saying
Do it again

How far a life can travel
in a single body!

No one you ever touched has left you,
though your hands have lived like butterflies

which do not recall each flower they drank from

You insist I sit in the fortune-teller's chair
We share a pot of mango tea,
nostalgia for paradise, for hell

Letter from Anywhere

The world has become a sheet of paper
covered with bright, jagged countries
on which I trace how far I am
from a place where I was known and held
in your two large hands.
Yet after days of eating, sleeping,
conversing in any common language,
a place grows fleshly, more similar
to all the other places.
At dusk I watch the people who belong here
cross the little bridge toward home.
The sky turns to granadilla.
Smoke from the foundry rises into fruity clouds,
making the same patterns smoke makes anywhere.
The roofs and trees, meanwhile,
are losing color;
when it grows dark enough they might forget themselves,
leave their posts,
sleep unburdened a few hours.
It is hard, always having to live
in the same body.
The people are fewer now.
I touch my own skin to remember yours.
High up the hill, cars move like bright-eyed animals,
traveling the ridged rim of the world
which they are defining, as they go,
making certain, by their solid presence,
that the land stays where it is,
not floating, or rising, or going home.
And I myself would love to go home,
though still I recognize that place most clearly

from a far distance.
The night is softer than I thought, not cold.
When all the light has been taken away,
the stars allow themselves to be seen.
I touch my skin, or someone else's, to remember yours.

Foreigner

—for Lee

Blond man in late-night restaurant, radiating
sex and fear—you pour me
beer, you lean close streaming plans and puckered
lips: a house on a Greek island. If you die,
you'll leave him something. If you live,

you'll be together always. Always
someday—not today, not now.
I've always been a foreigner, you say,
blowing a smoky kiss.
Are we in San Antonio? Seattle? Albuquerque? Our past

lives are pulsing, pushing through like poems
or needles, stitching disappearing maps.
Yes, you have begun to rust,
to wake in sweat which will not dry—
you who move through men like loose silk.

Still you want to shimmy out,
dive into some new country, deeper than a fuck.
Home is a place you've given up;
what I want is to meet you there,
to spend a long night in your smoke,

your rising, gold, endangered light.

In the Time of Plague

One night, my love, blond butterfly
cavorting in a mirrored room,
master of movement forward and backward
at the same time,
you told me the story of the Black
beautiful Brazilian priest
who huddled by the fire in his dark coat
big around him like the wings of a beetle

and when he took you, finally, into his room
and he undressed the sacrament, his flesh,
it was putrid, oozing, racked with sores,
even the cock, which first appeared unmarred,
haloed under the head with little festerings,
and there he stood with a shy smile
waiting to give himself to you
as if touch could say to the body,

you are absolutely perfect,
every molecule of you is perfect.
Afterward you gave him all your AZT,
stepped out into the glittering street.
In winter, after weeks of rain,
months of rain, so much it seems the sky will never stop
  shattering with mourning,
the body is a raven, stealing everything,
taking every shining thread for its nest.

You said, *I see myself in the mirror*
and I think, all this will disappear.

IN ANOTHER COUNTRY

1

There are houses climbing the sides of the volcano,
others spreading their pale roofs like paper birds
at its base to feed,
there is the evidence of other peoples' lives,
the lit paths of their roads and windows,
lines of clothing hung to dry
like flags from all the countries still unknown to you.

The sky is growing larger.
Possibly it will turn to water
and the trees to balsa rafts,
or it will turn to fire
and the trees will burn.
Clouds drift downhill like sheep,
eating everything.

And in this room, small, but with large windows,
you have decided to remake your life,
as if you could reach your hands into the oracle of your body
and place each organ on a different shelf,
by the force of will.

You are fused atoms, you are falling stars.

2

¡Somos una luz, caminando! shouts the streetcorner priest.
We are a light, walking.
Do you remember how it felt to realize
your life was not housed entirely in your body
but existed also outside of you
in some design or plan you would never fathom?

How you grew large then, with responsibility;
how you floated, bodiless, unmoored.

3

She is dancing, the little girl, maybe three years old,
around her waist the native *traje*, coarse, dark-blue,
and looped around her neck, beads of tradition: gold, blown glass
and you want to steal her

Her men, uncles, brothers stomp and laugh
making music come from their instruments and fingers
black hair like fields of black corn

and you think of the penis of each one,
guarded inside the pants like a thick, chopped stem

The tiny girl belongs completely
to her world—which you can never touch

We grow within the walls we are born to
They determine everything

Only, because she is so small,
she appears changeable—as if she still could be transplanted

This is what you want to steal:
the ability you think she has
to grow a new life

4

You return again and again to the truths of the body,
the only truths you know are shared.

In the church, you do not think of God,
only the thick, shining hair of the believing women,

religion like the shaping walls
of one's own name:
something they can be known by,
without questioning.

Even the boy with twisted, jerking limbs—
his hand redeems itself,
drawing the sign of the cross from navel to sternum,
nipple to nipple, the seeing eyes of the flesh.

5

The bus eats through hills of fog, traversing frightened roads
You lean further into the bodies of strangers
The country spreads itself before you as you pass

the women in the fields, still as clay figures in bright ponchos,
carved in shades of tangerine and fuschia from the green,
devouring, indifferent hills,

the fields of drought, where corn dulls on the helpless stalks,
the flooded streets, where children float on bicycles,

the river so certain of where it is going,
dividing, without intention, rich from poor,
and streaming obligingly over the soiled clothes
of the poor, which then are spread, a drying banquet of color,
along its shores,

the opened purple blouse of the woman next to you,
the dreaming child's lips held to the breast.

Because you are a foreigner, these things are beautiful.

Even in the seeing, your own life
does not relinquish you.

6

Now rain falls as if through a sieve,
scattering itself over all the land at once.

Missing someone, your body reaches across continents,
more faithful than you had thought possible.

Once, you believed equal
all cities, lovers, rainy nights.
You sat in your dark car of longing,
wanting everything larger, more significant,
wanting to look through the lit window
of someone else's life, and not your own—
as if everything you had made yours
was therefore limited, suspect, confining.
You wanted to fall freely, like rain, and alone.

You did not know that love could choose you,
that a city could hold you.
You thought all the choices were yours.

7

All evening lightning has shaken the sky with its dry,
panicking, promising sheets of white,
and new, small streams have created themselves
which were not here this afternoon,

but flow now with utter confidence and urgency
into the great awaiting river
while thunder hoarsely contemplates
overturning the world.

You left a light on in your room
and from here, far down the beach,
where your feet feel in the dark
for the land which receives you,
you watch it burning.

8

Memory rises where it will,
body of light summoned by thunder

Somewhere, there is a city
in which you will never be lost

Somewhere, fog drags its whole,
light, pinking body

over the hills, over the knifing roofs,
to enter, silently and wholly, into the city it loves.

You never knew before a place could bear so much,
could hold its streets like hands
under the weight of gifts.

9

You left your country wanting to move through the world
the way a bird moves on the clear sky's body,

to find a body which would never say
to the soul, you are too heavy to carry,

to see your life across the wide, unsteady marsh,
small as a toy city, shining from afar.

This is how far you had to go
to hear the music of returning.

It comes from above, from all around you,
like light charting the course your body follows.

They hold you anyway, these streets.
They forgive your other destinations.

Late Monologue for a Traveler

―for Lee

It's his Castellano Spanish makes me think of you,
the t-h sound lisped in the sex words:
hathlo   verguentha
homeless in a moving country
prancing, blond and raw

But these lives are like dotted lines—I know
you know what I mean. It seems so arbitrary,
where we let them take us,
we who were never allowed to believe
in any single destination,

our faces in the morning mirrors no more comforting
than the faces of the strangers leaving our beds.
That morning you spoke of, slipping unnoticed from a man's room,
then in the crowded, nameless streets
feeling for the first time that you *belonged*—

I left the same room once,
waited at the station amid the doughnuts and early
commuters, and I was satisfied.
After all those years of standing still
while the landscape rearranged itself,
loving each place best once I had left it for the next,

how familiar it felt to find you
in the passionate act of disappearing, of being taken away.
How much we longed to come like strangers
to our own lives,
give up the language we grew up with,
the words we understood too well,

and those which had failed to reveal us.
Sometimes, even now, I watch myself in the act of leaving,
live as if leaving were imminent, or because it is,
and at the same time hear myself, in the body's
fleshy voice, saying things I never meant to say,
saying *I will always love you,* saying *yes*—

and the voice of the body does not lie,
but neither does it understand
it is only one of the voices, the others go on choralling
from some other shore

Listen, the words we didn't use then—we can't have them back.
They are living other lives, could not wait for us.
Only the fingers tremble slightly, remembering
what they held,
that place in the body where all travel ends

Cirque du Soleil

When you are driving at night through mountains
so dark that your car seems the only place
where thought and music and light exist,

and you think of all the other cars
on other roads, rocketing alone,

piloted by other drivers,
each one believing in their own existence,

each one as alive as you,
speeding forward through unseeing land,

you remember the gymnasts
and their tigers, how they danced,
how they made their bodies into stars.

There are things people cannot do;
you have watched people doing them.
What did they feel then, as they flew

without nets, without wings?

V

Possible

It is the breast I remember seeing,
the nipple pink and round, the lustrous flesh,
before I saw the woman had no arms
in the locker room. Her teeth were excellent,
tugging her blouse on,

but it is her breast I remember
when I see again how what is perfect
lives beside what is tragic and damaged,
how silence arcs between these two,
each making the other possible

In Guatemala

—for Lynda and Ned

The buzzards waiting in a tree
in all their silent wisdom, profoundly black,
pulling flesh from the small carcass of dog,
and the marigolds, called here *las flores de los muertos,*
spread wild on hillsides, powdering yellow as hard-boiled yolk
over the desperate, the impeccable fields,
the corn with its tall, dry knowledge
and the proud green bellies of cabbages,
and beyond them, the clouds amassing their textures
 of incredible promise,
and the hoarse afternoon voice of the rooster,
and the no and the no and the why not,
the sound of someone sanding, scraping the same wall
 over and over,
the *conferencista* with his lush, irrelevant document of human rights.
Extranjeros, we gather images,
something more to carry with us
like arteries and lungs, hair and fingernails,
those body parts which work and grow without intention,
because what we carry becomes both our way of surviving,
and our reason for it—
the garbage scattered in its brightest colors
over the few unplanted fields
by the wind which will gather all of us,
but has not gathered us yet,
and the yes and the yes and the possible songs,
and the insects ravenous in their body-hunger,
and the absolute tenacity of sight and of blindness
making their way together down the dusty road.

Language Lesson

You want to know how to say, in English,
Me gustaría tener una relación contigo—
crouching against the plaza wall,
your paintings spread between us like lost worlds.
Scenes of *las indígenas:*
women with babies slung on backs
kneel in the maize, stacking their squash like jewels.
Turquoise cacti crowd their hills
Their machetes cut sweet stripes
The fish in their clear water have gold gills
Even the yoked cows look wise and brave.
Here in *el zocalo,* the bare bulbs sting,
we slap at slow mosquitoes,
I repeat the words:
I would like to have a relationship with you—
trying to hear them just as sounds,
not meaningful. The way I hear
so many of your words.
At first you wanted simple things:
words for *cerveza, ella, él.*
But a new language means new life,
there can never be enough.
The word *ciruela* fills my mouth full as the
thing, plum, itself. I want that ripe
dark bursting in me—everything I could not
say till now.

Almolonga Market

The man stooped almost to his knees
with the wide, shallow basket roped to his back

The basket, piled with calla lilies
Throats smudged honey-yellow
The hundreds of pale, fluted, luminous necks—

Is it different to carry weight in the form of beauty?
In their weight, do the flowers cease to be beautiful?

Or perhaps they remain beautiful, but the beauty no longer matters,
the fact of it simply floating, balloonlike, in the gray air,
next to the balloon of suffering,
as if the two were filled with the same wind,

or perhaps this is how beauty matters most,
common as leeks, carrots, cabbages—its inedible, essential blooms
neither harder nor easier to carry

History

How do you say *I am of a race smelted,*
the grief of metals forced,
the plundered and the plunderer
born of *el derecho de primera noche,*
the landowner passing the first night
with each of his workers' brides?
The old man said it this way:
we humans have no souls,
only instincts,
reacciones químicas.

But art, music, poetry?
Yes—flutes fashioned from human femurs,
from the donkey's jaw,
rattles from amputated hooves of sheep,
strings stretched across the killed armadillo's back.
It is said that Hitler loved music.
Always we have craved the abstract glittering
beyond our animal selves,
and we have murdered to achieve it
as if beauty would rise phoenixlike
not from ashes, but from pooled blood,
dripped like holy water through the fingers
at the dark mouth of the mine.
Four months without daylight!
How do you say: I am of the horse,
and those who whipped the horse
dead on the eighth day;
I am of the miner, and those who savagely bandaged

the miner's eyes, when he emerged,
because he would have been less useful blind?
How do you live an ordinary life
hanging the bleached sheets to dry
against the great, green volcano of history,

while still the human eye searches for beauty,
following the curves of land,
the cross-grained valleys, gingerbread-clay roofs,
the lone, speckled rooster on his garbage heap,
the fog laying its silky hands over the volcano's peaks
softly, but entirely,
the stone, chiseled faces of the statues erected over cadavers
in each city park,
the legless cripples, twisting crablike between tables
in the sidewalk cafés, holding up their hands.

There is a way to see without condemning.
Nothing human is alien to me,
said the Jew who studied Hitler as his life's work.

It is said there are parents
who cripple their children, so they will be able to eat.

High on the hill, where open sewers run like a blood current,
swallows flap their rapid wings
over the childrens' muddy ball games, as if blessing them;

women emerge from doorways, holding cloth, buckets, soap;
the untended grass grows lush,
the rooster crows in anguish or triumph,
hoarsely certain of everything
under a masterpiece of clouds, fog, sudden bits of blue,
the blinding, gifting sun.
In this language, *sky* and *heaven* are the same word.
The old man said *we are soulless, we are chemical reactions,*
but reverence is not a chemical reaction;
nor is hope, which, unfettered by gravity,
extends itself over the valleys of our lives.
And unlike instincts, which serve to keep us alive,
this vision will not save us,
will not save even our souls (if we have them),
which, by the time they rise to heaven or sky
have been tainted by understanding
more than they ever meant to understand
(nothing human is alien to me)—
which is why this magnificent hilltop
has been consigned to house the poor,
because from here you can see everything,
and those who can will pay to not see.

The wings of the swallows are pure white
against the spaces opened by the cliff,
and they traverse so easily
what is forbidden us, a species land-condemned,
moving in perfect groups
as if, by invisible signal,
they could choose to share a single heart,
effortlessly bridging the vast space of self,

❖

and of course they are not praying for us
but only wondering about the broken wings
of the plastic bags, the garbage fluttering whitely
where we let it fall.
I am of the plundered and the plunderer.
It is turquoise, the woman's shawl,
her bucket orange, the soap pink,
the ball bounced by the children black and white,
the rooster red and green and mottled gold.

There is a way to see.

—*Quito, Ecuador*

The Twelfth Day of Christmas

Inside the domed basilica,
beneath flaming honeycomb windows,
the endless reenactment in the straw,

hands over heart, knees to the bench,
on *el dia de los reyes,* day of the wise men
bearing gifts,

your voice is harnessed to the ancient
sled of human effort,
all of the voices rising, wing above wing,
guided like birds or promises
through the still air,

the music like a human child
which must be borne through the body,

and the body magnificent as a church
in all its failures,
the huge, pink eyes of the breasts
cast downward,
the belly thrust out from its cage of bone,

the body which is not only
birds, not only the thin, delicate
whorled cartilage of the ears,
but which is also mouth and genitals,
rooting us to the earth,

and how the meat of the body
gives of itself!—

now, as it shudders into song.

Late Summer

Walking the earth in all the changing
weather of our bodies
Days like Indian corn, their kernels
amber, ruby, jade

Lugging around these bodies, awkward as potato sacks,
a giant's boots, stumbling through the fields
picking raspberries

The fruits fall whole into our hands
They do not grieve

The sugars in your body, rising like a tide
Your baby skin, your old woman's breasts
The wild vanilla of your breath
Your blood's jewel on the white slide
of the glucometer

I think the soul must love the flesh
like we love fireworks,
for brief extravagance, for lighting up the sky
with their disappearing: rubies everywhere

The Greatest Show on Earth

—Barnum and Bailey Circus, 1994

The gorgeous senselessness of it,
fifteen elephants with battered saggy hides
draped with sequinned cloths
Lined up trunk to tail, they rise
placing their enormous hooves
on each others' backs;
some of them open their blind mouths

¡Míralo, está dando vueltas!
The bear is turning and turning
on the horse's back
The bear unadorned, no glittering
costume for him, only the brown
jiggling animal haunches
The bear, who has no fingers, swaying to hold on
through the speeding trot

And what the acrobats do
with their human bodies!
The womens' pale legs open scissor wide
on the high wire,
their thighs are dripping flame
Men walk the rope, feet on each others'
shoulders, balanced spears of light

The one long note which is grief sustaining
all the music
The effort seen on any one face
Violin shrugging upward, the brassy tuba
blaring out its sequence like a flag

lofted over all the hungers
Because there is always a journey, always difficult
Accordion breathing and dancing, your body
never refuses song

Ruth L. Schwartz

was born in Geneva, New York, in 1962, and spent her childhood and early adulthood moving around the country. She left home at sixteen, received a B.A. from Wesleyan University in 1983 and an M.F.A. in creative writing from the University of Michigan in 1985. She now lives in Oakland, California, with her partner, Gladys, and a houseful of pets.

Ms. Schwartz worked as an AIDS educator for eight years, and still works in the field of health education. She has also traveled extensively in Latin America.

She has been the recipient of fellowships from the National Endowment for the Arts and the Astraea Foundation, as well as numerous awards from literary journals.

Acknowledgments

The author and publisher wish to acknowledge the following publications in which some of these poems first appeared, some in slightly different versions: *Americas Review* ("The City"); *Artful Dodge* ("Letter from Anywhere," "Scene with Pelicans"); *Chelsea* ("The City at Sunset," "The Greatest Show on Earth"); *Madison Review* ("When They Know"); *Nimrod* ("Finally, there is your lust," "I keep coming back to this longing," "The man speaks," "Poems of the Body," "When you in your sturdy and luminous body"); *Northwest Poets and Artists' 1995 Calendar* ("Late Summer"); *Parnassus: Poetry in Review* ("History"); *Provincetown Arts* ("And the Light"); *S. F. Bay Guardian* ("The City"); *Southern California Anthology* ("AIDS Education, Seventh Grade"); *Southwest Review* ("The Offering," "Late Monologue for a Traveler"); *Sow's Ear Review* ("Late Summer"); *Taos Review* ("By Asking"); and *Zone Three* ("The City").

"Near us, a new house," "Possible," and "In Guatemala" originally appeared in *New Letters,* Winter 1992 (Volume 58, Number 2). They are reprinted here with the permission of *New Letters* and the curators of the University of Missouri–Kansas City.

I am grateful to the Centrum Foundation for a residency which allowed me to begin configuring this manuscript, and to the Astraea Foundation and the National Endowment for the Arts for grants which were of great help in the book's final stages.

I could never have written these poems if my life had not been touched and transformed by the spirit, love, and insight of far more people than I can name. Special gratitude goes to Héctor and Na'ama, and my writer-friends, particularly Julia (who claims to have read this manuscript more times than anyone else alive), Alison, and Sheryl. I was moved and inspired, always, by the volunteers of the San Francisco AIDS Foundation and the San Mateo County AIDS Program. I thank my family for accepting the poet in their midst, and my mother for her unflagging support of my writing. Above all, I am grateful to Gladys, who has infused my life and my poetry with passion.

PITT POETRY SERIES

Ed Ochester, General Editor

Claribel Alegría, *Flowers from the Volcano*
Claribel Alegría, *Woman of the River*
Debra Allbery, *Walking Distance*
Maggie Anderson, *Cold Comfort*
Maggie Anderson, *A Space Filled with Moving*
Dorothy Barresi, *The Post-Rapture Diner*
Jan Beatty, *Mad River*
Robin Becker, *Giacometti's Dog*
Siv Cedering, *Letters from the Floating World*
Lorna Dee Cervantes, *Emplumada*
Robert Coles, *A Festering Sweetness: Poems of American People*
Billy Collins, *The Art of Drowning*
Nancy Vieira Couto, *The Face in the Water*
Jim Daniels, *M-80*
Kate Daniels, *The Niobe Poems*
Kate Daniels, *The White Wave*
Toi Derricotte, *Captivity*
Sharon Doubiago, *South America Mi Hija*
Stuart Dybek, *Brass Knuckles*
Odysseus Elytis, *The Axion Esti*
Jane Flanders, *Timepiece*
Forrest Gander, *Lynchburg*
Richard Garcia, *The Flying Garcias*
Suzanne Gardinier, *The New World*
Gary Gildner, *Blue Like the Heavens: New & Selected Poems*
Elton Glaser, *Color Photographs of the Ruins*
Hunt Hawkins, *The Domestic Life*
Lawrence Joseph, *Curriculum Vitae*
Lawrence Joseph, *Shouting at No One*
Julia Kasdorf, *Sleeping Preacher*
Etheridge Knight, *The Essential Etheridge Knight*
Bill Knott, *Poems, 1963–1988*
Ted Kooser, *One World at a Time*
Ted Kooser, *Sure Signs: New and Selected Poems*
Ted Kooser, *Weather Central*
Larry Levis, *The Widening Spell of the Leaves*
Larry Levis, *Winter Stars*
Larry Levis, *Wrecking Crew*
Walter McDonald, *Counting Survivors*
Irene McKinney, *Six O'Clock Mine Report*
Archibald MacLeish, *The Great American Fourth of July Parade*
Peter Meinke, *Liquid Paper: New and Selected Poems*

Peter Meinke, *Night Watch on the Chesapeake*
Carol Muske, *Applause*
Carol Muske, *Wyndmere*
Leonard Nathan, *Carrying On: New & Selected Poems*
Kathleen Norris, *Little Girls in Church*
Ed Ochester and Peter Oresick, *The Pittsburgh Book of Contemporary American Poetry*
Sharon Olds, *Satan Says*
Gregory Orr, *City of Salt*
Alicia Suskin Ostriker, *Green Age*
Alicia Suskin Ostriker, *The Imaginary Lover*
Greg Pape, *Black Branches*
Greg Pape, *Storm Pattern*
Kathleen Peirce, *Mercy*
David Rivard, *Torque*
Liz Rosenberg, *Children of Paradise*
Liz Rosenberg, *The Fire Music*
Natasha Sajé, *Red Under the Skin*
Maxine Scates, *Toluca Street*
Ruth L. Schwartz, *Accordion Breathing and Dancing*
Robyn Selman, *Directions to My House*
Richard Shelton, *Selected Poems, 1969–1981*
Reginald Shepherd, *Some Are Drowning*
Betsy Sholl, *The Red Line*
Peggy Shumaker, *The Circle of Totems*
Peggy Shumaker, *Wings Moist from the Other World*
Jeffrey Skinner, *The Company of Heaven*
Cathy Song, *School Figures*
Leslie Ullman, *Dreams by No One's Daughter*
Constance Urdang, *Alternative Lives*
Constance Urdang, *Only the World*
Michael Van Walleghen, *Tall Birds Stalking*
Ronald Wallace, *People and Dog in the Sun*
Ronald Wallace, *Time's Fancy*
Belle Waring, *Refuge*
Michael S. Weaver, *My Father's Geography*
Michael S. Weaver, *Timber and Prayer: The Indian Pond Poems*
Robley Wilson, *Kingdoms of the Ordinary*
Robley Wilson, *A Pleasure Tree*
David Wojahn, *Glassworks*
David Wojahn, *Late Empire*
David Wojahn, *Mystery Train*
Paul Zimmer, *Family Reunion: Selected and New Poems*